A FRIENDLY GUIDE TO VATICAN II

MAX VODOLA

garratt PUBLISHING

Published in Australia by
Garratt Publishing
32 Glenvale Crescent
Mulgrave, Vic. 3170
www.garrattpublishing.com.au

Copyright © Max Vodola 2012

All rights reserved. Except as provided by the Australian copyright law, no part of this book may be reproduced in any way without permission in writing from the publisher.

Design by Lynne Muir

Text editing by Juliette Hughes

Images: Thinkstock

Copyright MDHC Catholic Archdiocese of Melbourne

Nihil Obstat: Reverend Monsignor Peter Kenny STD, Diocesan Censor

Imprimatur: Monsignor Greg Bennet, Vicar General

Date: 2 July 2012

The Nihil Obstat and Imprimatur are official declarations that a book or pamphlet is free of doctrinal or moral error. No implication is contained therein that those who have granted the Nihil Obstat and Imprimatur agree with the contents, opinions or statements expressed. They do not necessarily signify that the work is approved as a basic text for catechetical instruction.

9781921946301

Cataloguing in Publication information for this title is available from the National Library of Australia.

www.nla.gov.au

The author and publisher gratefully acknowledge the permission granted to reproduce the copyright material in this book. Every effort has been made to trace copyright holders and to obtain their permission for the use of copyright material. The publisher apologises for any errors or omissions in the above list and would be grateful if notified of any corrections that should be incorporated in future reprints or editions of this book.

Garratt Publishing has included on its website a page for special notices in relation to this and our other publications.

Please visit www.garrattpublishing.com.au

CONTENTS

CHAPTER 1	**HISTORICAL BACKGROUND**	3
	Councils in the Church	4
	Pope John XXIII	5
	Early Years	5
	As Priest	7
	As Bishop	8
	As Nuncio	10
	As Cardinal	12
	As Pope	12
CHAPTER 2	**CALLING THE COUNCIL (VATICAN II)**	14
	The first 100 Days	16
	The First Session of Vatican II	19
	Death of the Pope	21
	Further Sessions	22
	Vatican II – The Australian Contribution	23
	The Second Vatican Council: A Time line	26
CHAPTER 3	**IMPLEMENTING VATICAN II**	29
	Some major reforms of Vatican II	32
	Documents of Vatican II	33
CHAPTER 4	**THE CONTINUING DEBATES**	43
	Understanding the Council that changed our Lives	44
	The Nature of the Change	46

Chapter 1:

Historical Background

Councils in the Church

A Council is an occasional gathering of church representatives, mainly bishops, for the purpose of consultation and decision-making on important matters in the life of the Church. The Church teaches that such Councils are convoked under the inspiration of the Holy Spirit in order to determine issues relating to doctrine, dogma and theological practice binding on the whole church. The form, style, length and structure of Councils have varied greatly over the centuries, often in relation to the disputed theological issue which gave rise to the Council and the historical context of the time. Vatican II or the Second Vatican Council (1962–65) was designated the twenty-first Ecumenical Council, the first being Nicaea in 325. The early Councils of the Church concentrated largely on the 'Christological' controversies; that is, clarifying in a theological way the unity of Christ's humanity and divinity. The Creed that is recited at Mass on Sundays was formulated and refined in the course of these early Councils. A close study of Councils also reveals often fiery and lengthy debate over controversial and contentious issues in the life of the Church.

Rendering of Pope Pius IX addressing the First Vatican Council (1869)

DID YOU KNOW?

There have been twenty-one Ecumenical Councils in the history of the Church

1.	Nicaea I	325	13.	Lyons I	1245
2.	Constantinople I	381	14.	Lyons II	1274
3.	Ephesus	431	15.	Vienne	1311
4.	Chalcedon	451	16.	Constance	1414–18
5.	Constantinople II	553	17.	Florence	1431–45
6.	Constantinople III	680	(also known as Basel-Ferrara-Florence-Rome)		
7.	Nicaea II	787			
8.	Constantinople IV	869	18.	Lateran V	1512–17
9.	Lateran I	1123	19.	Trent	1545–63
10.	Lateran II	1139	20.	Vatican I	1869–70
11.	Lateran III	1179	21.	Vatican II	1962–65
12.	Lateran IV	1215			

POPE JOHN XXIII

EARLY YEARS

Angelo Giuseppe Roncalli was born on 25 November 1881 in the small village of Sotto il Monte in Bergamo, in northern Italy. He was the fourth of eleven children and the first son to his parents who were local tenant farmers. By all accounts, the young Angelo had an unremarkable upbringing. Later, as pope, Roncalli would recall with affection the relative poverty, humility and simplicity of his early years. His primary education was in the local village school. Expressing a desire for the priesthood, Angelo was then sent to the minor seminary in Bergamo; he followed this with studies in Rome.

As a teenage seminarian, Roncalli commenced what would become his great spiritual testament, *Journal of a Soul*, and he remained faithful in maintaining this journal throughout his life, including his relatively short papacy. Much in the journal is consistent with many of the images of him when he was pope – kind, benign, humble, open-hearted, faithful to his Christian calling and priestly commitment, and eager to do the will of God by following the example of the saints. On the surface, *Journal of a Soul* reflects the spirituality of the time in a young aspirant to the priesthood – resolutions regarding prayer and fasting, going to confession, praying the rosary, visits to the Blessed Sacrament and examination of conscience. However, the journal also reflects the intersection in Roncalli between spiritual development and intellectual formation, his capacity to reflect on his experience in the light of Christian history and his ability to situate himself within the context of some of the burning questions and issues of the day.

Roncalli arrived in Rome early in 1901 (aged nineteen) to complete his studies for the priesthood. There was great intellectual and theological ferment in Rome at this time due to the use of what is known as the 'historical-critical' method of biblical studies which was widely used in Protestant circles but frowned upon by the Catholic Church. The young Roncalli was surrounded by professors and fellow students who wanted the Catholic Church to embrace with vigour this critical study of the bible and theology. The 'would-be' historian expressed some cautious openness to these ideas and entries in *Journal of a Soul* reveal moments of deep spiritual and intellectual struggle:

> My study shall always be in all sacred sciences and in all questions of a theological or biblical nature to investigate first the traditional doctrine of the Church and on this basis to judge the findings of contemporary scholarship. I do not despise critical thought and I shall be most careful not to think ill of critics or treat them with disrespect. On the contrary, I love critical thought, I shall be glad to keep up with the most recent findings, I shall study the new systems of thought and their continual evolution and their trends; criticism for me is light, is truth, and there is only one truth which is sacred.

Here we see evidence of how Roncalli in his journey to the priesthood was being shaped by some of the wider historical, theological and cultural shifts in Catholicism which was a source of some tension in the Church. While Pope Pius X rejected any sense of openness towards the historical-critical approach to theology and the scriptures, this time of struggle for Roncalli planted a seed in the heart of the would-be historian. His reflections and writings show how Roncalli was interpreting the reality of *change* in his own life and in the life of the Church.

Bergamo Italy, birthpace of Roncalli

As Priest

Roncalli was ordained to the priesthood in Rome on 10 August 1904. There was speculation that he would remain in Rome to continue higher studies in canon law, but the appointment of a new bishop to Bergamo changed all that. Giacomo Radini Tedeschi (1857–1914) was consecrated Bishop of Bergamo personally by Pope Pius X in the Sistine Chapel on 29 January 1905. Roncalli assisted at the ceremony and was later chosen to be the personal secretary of the new bishop. On his return to Bergamo, Roncalli was occupied in two main tasks: lecturer at the diocesan seminary in history, patristics and apologetics and secretary to Tedeschi. The new bishop modelled for his secretary something that would be essential to Roncalli's later career: an emphasis on the bishop as pastor and shepherd, attentive to the needs of his flock and seeking to bring about necessary adaptation that would later reveal something of the reason for calling Vatican II:

> There had been no synod in Bergamo since 1724 – a gap of nearly two hundred years – so the occasion had special significance. The mass of old and new diocesan legislation which had been found here and there in innumerable documents, instructions, traditions and local customs was revised, brought into line with the needs of modern times and altered circumstances and given new and authoritative confirmation.
>
> A.G. Roncalli, *My Bishop: A Portrait of Mgr. Giacomo Maria Radini Tedeschi*. (Translated by D White). London: Geoffrey Chapman, 1969, p. 92.

The phrase 'revised and brought into line with the needs of modern times' is a key phrase from the early writings of Roncalli that help us to understand how history was shaping his perspective on the life and mission of the Church. The word *'aggiornamento'*

> CRITICISM FOR ME IS LIGHT, IS TRUTH,
> AND THERE IS ONLY ONE TRUTH
> WHICH IS SACRED.

and renewal of the diocese in the face of new and changing historical realities.

In order to familiarise himself with his new diocese, Tedeschi commenced a prodigious and extensive program of pastoral visitation of the diocese of Bergamo, which at that time numbered approximately 350 parishes. Working alongside the bishop, Roncalli began to develop an understanding of the essential link between pastoral activity and the process of renewal in the Church. The pastoral visitation culminated in a diocesan synod which was held in 1910. As secretary of the bishop, Roncalli was also appointed official secretary of the synod and charged with publication of the relevant documents. In a biography published soon after Tedeschi's death in 1914, Roncalli spoke of the synod as 'the most solemn and important event of his episcopate … a source of intense joy'. It is important to note the way Roncalli framed his ideas historically and shaped a form of language (bringing up to date) would later be used at Vatican II as a word associated with John XXIII.

As Roncalli threw himself into his work as seminary lecturer and bishop's secretary, he also found time to research and publish articles in the local Catholic journal *La Vita Diocesana* on the previous bishops of Bergamo, the various diocesan synods and other items of local history. But it was a chance discovery at this time that would engage Roncalli's historical interest over a lifetime and which would shape his vision and language as pope in calling the Second Vatican Council. On a trip to Milan in 1906 with Tedeschi, Roncalli took himself off to the diocesan archives and made an accidental discovery. He found 39 volumes of original material related to Borromeo's apostolic visitation to Bergamo in 1575 in the wake of the Council of Trent. The material was marked *'Archivio Spirituale – Bergamo'*. Roncalli wrote:

I was immediately struck by the collection of 39 parchment volumes which I discovered and explored in great detail on subsequent visits. What a pleasant surprise to find bound together such a copious and interesting collection of documents on the Church in Bergamo in a period of characteristic renewal following the Council of Trent …

A.G. Roncalli, Gli Atti della Visita Apostolica di San Carlo Borromeo a Bergamo (1575). Vol 1. Firenze: Olschki, 1936

Roncalli brought this material to the bishop's attention; the bishop then established a special commission to photograph, transcribe and edit this material. There were big plans underway for numerous publications. However by 1914 Tedeschi was dead and the First World War was about to break out. The new bishop of Bergamo showed little interest in this work and the commission was disbanded. But Roncalli held onto the material and also to the dream of one day seeing it published.

As Bishop

In the early 1920s, Roncalli left Bergamo and was called to Rome where he was appointed National Director of the Missions. He seemed to enjoy this work of travelling around Italy and raising funds. However, he was greatly shocked in 1925 when he was informed that Pope Pius XI (1922–39) had selected him as Apostolic Visitor to Bulgaria. Roncalli had not undertaken any formal training as a papal diplomat and was to be consecrated a bishop for the purposes of this new ministry. His association with Pius XI (Achille Ratti) was quite fortuitous. Ratti had been prefect of the Ambrosian Library in Milan and was an expert librarian, linguist and archivist. It was Ratti who both supervised and gave expert advice to the young Roncalli in copying, transcribing and editing Borromeo's 1575 apostolic visitation to Bergamo.

Council of Trent (1545-63)

Roncalli was consecrated a bishop on 19 March 1925 at the church of San Carlo in Rome. He set off to a largely unknown country with a very small and scattered Catholic population, vastly different from the world of Bergamo and Rome that had been familiar to him. But this important period in his life demonstrated an essential and endearing feature of Roncalli's personality – openness to new ideas, new experiences, new times and new historical circumstances. Roncalli's task in Bulgaria was to assess local conditions for the Church and report back to Rome. He thought his mission would last about six months and that he would then be moved elsewhere either to a diocese of his own in Italy or to a more prestigious diplomatic appointment elsewhere. As the time passed, Roncalli's diary and letters home hint at a certain sense of 'languishing' in Bulgaria. However, he had always trusted in God's will for his life, and had sworn obedience to the Pope. During his time in Bulgaria, Roncalli began to finesse his own pastoral style of ministry, modelled very much on the historical figure of Borromeo and the example of Tedeschi. He made numerous visits to victims of a tragic earthquake in 1928 and made available relief aid to Catholics and non-Catholics alike which made a favourable impression on civic authorities. As a young bishop, Roncalli constantly made reference to the essentially 'pastoral' nature of his ministry as a papal diplomat. In a letter to his superiors in Rome, Roncalli spoke of 'the new era for the Catholic Church in the Orient …a sign of the times'. Roncalli often worked towards positive, warm and friendly relations with the various branches of the Orthodox tradition and other non-Catholic communities, seeking to avoid the use of harsh language such as 'heretics' and 'schismatics'.

St Charles Borromeo (1538-1584)

Did you know?

During his time in Bulgaria, Roncalli spoke with great warmth and affection on the issue of ecumenism which became a hallmark of Vatican II.

> I offer greetings and best wishes also to our separated Orthodox brothers (and sisters), separated from us because of diverse disciplinary reasons, but joined to us in the same adoration of Father, Son and Holy Spirit…that one day, not too far from now, we will see ourselves united in the participation of peace and joy that the Holy Spirit, the Paraclete, pours out incessantly on the Catholic Church…
>
> Bulgaria, Feast of Pentecost, May 1925.

As Nuncio

In 1934, Roncalli was advised by the Holy See that his new diplomatic posting would be to Turkey and Greece. He remained there throughout the Second World War and became known for his friendly and open attitude to non-Catholic Christians and adherents to the Muslim and Jewish faith. It was during this time that Roncalli re-commenced the work of editing the historical material on Borromeo that had been left in abeyance two decades previously. In the slow and time-consuming task of editing this material, often late into the night, Roncalli started to see some parallels between Borromeo's pastoral reform of the Church in the wake of Trent in the sixteenth century and Roncalli's diplomatic and pastoral ministry in the changing circumstances of the early twentieth century. Just as the Church – in the wake of Trent – had to adapt to new circumstances and bring about pastoral reform and renewal, Roncalli discerned for himself a similar need and pattern as he went about the business of papal diplomacy and extensive pastoral visitation which he described as 'the principal act of my ministry'.

In a remarkable burst of energy, Roncalli was able to publish three dense volumes of Borromeo's visitation titled *The Acts of the Apostolic Visitation of St Charles Borromeo to Bergamo (1575)*. The Introduction to Volume 1 published in 1936 deserves particular attention. In describing the pastoral renewal instigated by Trent and practiced by Borromeo, Roncalli describes this period as 'a fruitful rejuvenation of the Church ... a vigourous regaining of Catholic life ... an awakening of such potent energy not known in any other period of the Church'. Roncalli reserves a special place for Borromeo whom he praises for being a model bishop 'extending the benefits of his prodigious reforming activity throughout the parishes of the region'. Borromeo is recognised for his pastoral zeal and his ability to meet 'the new needs of the time'.

In 1944, Roncalli was transferred to the prestigious diplomatic post of Paris. He had now entered the upper echelons of Vatican diplomacy. But this promotion did not radically change the priest born of humble origins. Roncalli's diary for this period shows consistent references to the essentially 'pastoral' nature of his diplomatic ministry, his dynamic view of history and his sense that the Church and the world were entering 'new times'. At over sixty years of age, Roncalli would work late into the night (and while on holidays in Italy) to complete the fourth volume of Borromeo's visitation which was published in 1946. This constant intersection between pastoral ministry and historical reflection continued when in 1953 Roncalli was appointed Patriarch of Venice.

Did you know?

Prior to the Council of Trent, bishops had charge of numerous dioceses.

Many bishops hardly ever stepped foot in their various dioceses but would leave the administration to delegates and other curial officials.

Trent mandated that a bishop was to have charge of only one diocese, that he was to reside in that diocese, that he was to regularly visit the parishes of that diocese and that he was to establish a seminary for the proper formation of the clergy.

DID YOU KNOW?

It was at the diocesan synod in Venice in 1957 that Roncalli first used the word '*aggiornamento*'?

Haven't you heard the word 'aggiornamento' repeated many times? Here is our Church, always young and ready to follow the different changes in the circumstances of life, with the intention of adapting, correcting, improving, and arousing enthusiasm. In summary, this is the nature of the synod: this is its purpose.

St Mark's Venice

HISTORICAL BACKGROUND

As Cardinal

In 1953 Roncalli was appointed Patriarch of Venice. He was conscious that he now had what he had always wanted – the direct care of souls as a diocesan bishop. He commenced a prodigious round of pastoral visitation, describing himself constantly as the 'shepherd' and 'pastor' of the diocese. The extensive pastoral visitation of the diocese culminated in a diocesan synod in 1957. Once again we find Roncalli using a form of words that would reach their peak at Vatican II.

As Pope

In 1958, Pope Pius XII died after an eighteen year reign. Prior to leaving for Rome, Roncalli wrote in his diary, 'The grace of the Lord is always with his Church. We are not here on earth to look after a museum but to cultivate a flourishing garden of life and to prepare for a glorious future. The Pope is dead. Long live the Pope'. There was much speculation in Rome about a successor and it was at this time that talk emerged of a 'transitional' or 'caretaker' pope, one who would simply keep

Pope John XXIII

the wheels of the Vatican bureaucracy in motion without introducing any abrupt policy changes for the Church. Roncalli was seen as that candidate – friendly, warm, harmless, genial, a relatively obscure and uncontroversial figure in the world of papal diplomacy and a respected bishop during his brief time in Venice.

Following his election on 28 October 1958, the Church and the world were immediately struck by the contrast of the new pope with his predecessor. There were many surprises. The first was the choice of name. The Church had had four 'Pius' popes in one hundred years. It was felt that the tradition would continue. When Roncalli announced the name 'John', it took many by surprise. He stated that he chose 'John' because it was the name of his father and the name of the humble parish of his baptism. He also stated that it was the name of innumerable basilicas around the world, including his own Lateran Basilica as Bishop of Rome. He went on, 'It was the name of the long series of Roman Pontiffs, all of whom had a short pontificate'.

The Church really had not been used to a newly elected pope speaking so warmly and intimately about his father and the humble parish of his baptism. If his choice of name indicated a new way of thinking for the Church, it was the first of many innovations. In receiving the customary sign of respect from the cardinals following his election, John XXIII insisted that the custom of kissing the pontiff's feet, a gesture that had imperial overtones, be eliminated forthwith.

Whereas Pius XII had appeared regal, stern and somewhat detached, John XXIII impressed many by his warm and down to earth character. The new pope attempted to rid the Vatican of some of the exaggerated imperial overtones that had surrounded the papal office. As he began his new ministry, he gave subtle hints about the style of papacy he would follow. He spoke of being a shepherd and going out in search of the lost sheep. He directed that his papal coronation was to be held on a feast-day dear to his heart – 4 November, the feast of St Charles Borromeo. The fifth and final volume of the *Atti* was published soon after Roncalli was elected pope.

St Peter's in Rome

Angelo Giuseppe Roncalli

1881 Born on 25 November in the small village of Sotto il Monte in Bergamo, in northern Italy

As a teenage seminarian, Roncalli commenced what would become his great spiritual testament: *Journal of a Soul*

1901 Arrived in Rome (aged nineteen) to complete his studies for the priesthood

1904 Ordained to the priesthood in Rome on 10 August

1920s Left Bergamo and called to Rome and appointed National Director of the Missions

1925 Selected by Pope Pius XI to be Apostolic Visitor to Bulgaria

1925 Consecrated a bishop on 19 March at the church of San Carlo in Rome.

1934 Advised by the Holy See that his new diplomatic posting would be to Turkey and Greece.

1944 Transferred to the prestigious diplomatic post of Paris

1953 Appointed Patriarch of Venice.

1958 Following his election on 28 October 1958, the Church and the world were immediately struck by the contrast of the new pope with his predecessor

1962 The first session of the Council met from 11 October until 8 December 1962

1963 Pope John XXIII died on 3 June 1963

Chapter 2:
Calling the Council (Vatican II)

The first 100 Days

In contemporary political discourse, much is made of a new leader's 'first 100 days'. Journalists and political pundits are often on the lookout for a new leader's change of direction or major policy shift. The Roman Curia were just beginning to get used to the new and less formal style of John XXIII when a surprise announcement shocked many. It was 25 January 1959, the feast of the conversion of St Paul. John XXIII had just presided at the ceremony to close the Week of Prayer for Christian Unity, an observance dear to his heart from his time in the Orient. Despite the sometimes frosty ecumenical relations before Vatican II, Rome observed this occasion with some formality. Following the celebration, John XXIII gathered a group of approximately twenty cardinals to the chapter house of the nearby Benedictine monastery of St Paul Outside the Walls. It was then that John XXIII dropped what could only be described as a bombshell. The newly elected pope spoke as an historian, a shepherd and a friend:

> I am prompted to open my mind and heart to you and to tell you frankly about several points

Opening of Council's 2nd Session Vatican II, United Press Photos London, © MDHC Catholic Archdiocese of Melbourne

of planned pastoral activity which have emerged in my thoughts. In doing so, I am thinking of the care of the souls of the faithful in these modern times. I am gradually settling into my new role and beginning to see how it will fit into the overall history of the Church ... So now, trembling a bit with emotion, I announce to you my intention to hold a twofold event: a diocesan wide meeting for this city and an ecumenical Council for the universal Church. And this will also lead to a bringing up-to-date of the code of canon law which will accompany and crown these two events ... We think this will produce a great enlightenment for all Christian people as well as a renewed invitation to our separated brothers and sisters.

Pope John was later to remark that his announcement was met by the cardinals with 'stony silence'. Once the news was made public, there was some confusion and uncertainty about the precise reason and exact nature of this 'Council'. Vatican I, which enshrined the doctrine of papal infallibility, was suspended in 1870 in an atmosphere of crisis following the overthrow of the papal states. Councils from centuries ago had often met to discuss contentious and divisive theological viewpoints in the Church. There seemed to be no prevailing crisis in the Church which required the attention of a Council in 1959, hence the surprise at Pope John's announcement. But his language gave away some important clues. Vatican II was to be a Council of renewal and 'updating' (*aggiornamento*) with a particular focus of reaching out to 'our separated brothers and sisters' in the Christian faith.

Preparing the Council was a massive undertaking. Senior figures in the Roman Curia wanted to send out a formulated questionnaire to the bishops of the world. Pope John insisted that the bishops were to be totally free to suggest items or major themes for discussion at the Council. Many bishops sought out the advice of theologians, seminary rectors and ecclesiastical academics. A number of these scholars gave advice that built on many decades of research and scholarship in theology and pastoral practice. For example, many promoted a more historical and critical understanding of the scriptures, enhanced and better liturgical participation through changes to the Mass such as the vernacular and the priest turning to face the people. There were ideas such as the promotion of an authentic and distinctive lay spirituality based on baptism, better dialogue and interaction with non-Catholic and non-Christian people. This process of worldwide consultation and the assembling of preparatory 'schemas' took almost three years. Some less enlightened bishops wanted the Council to condemn and denounce the threat of communism, to issue new Marian decrees and to address technical points of canon law. The logistical arrangements were just as complex as the theological ones. Rome was on standby to receive over 2,000 bishops from around the world, their secretaries and advisers and a large international media that with the advent of television began to take a very serious interest in this major gathering of Catholic bishops.

After almost four years of intense preparation, Vatican II commenced on 11 October 1962. Prior to the official start of proceedings, a long procession of bishops made their way into St Peter's Basilica. Many observers were struck not simply by the sheer number of bishops but by the diversity of their background and appearance. There were bishops from Asia, Africa and Latin America, bishops from the various Eastern rite and Oriental traditions of the Catholic Church: – Melkites, Maronites, Ukrainians, Chaldeans, Syro-Malabar, Coptic and Armenian.

> I ANNOUNCE TO YOU MY INTENTION TO HOLD A TWOFOLD EVENT:
> A DIOCESAN WIDE MEETING FOR THIS CITY AND AN
> ECUMENICAL COUNCIL FOR THE UNIVERSAL CHURCH.

At the end of the procession came John XXIII carried on the *sedia gestatoria* (gestatorial chair). He looked somewhat worried and pensive. There were many disagreements in the Church just to get to this point, especially concerning the wording of almost seventy preparatory schemata. Many did not know that John XXIII had been diagnosed with stomach cancer, hence the possible anxiety that he was starting something that he would not live long enough to complete. After stepping down from the throne, Pope John intoned the hymn to the Holy Spirit, Mass was celebrated in Latin, the bishops recited the Profession of Faith and carried out their rite of obedience to the Pope and the Sistine Choir sang the Creed. Some bishops would have noticed the Book of the Gospels solemnly enthroned before them as had been done at previous Councils. Not only does this recall the sovereignty of Christ over the gathering but would also lead to Vatican II's new appreciation of the place of the word of God in the life of the Church. After almost three hours of various liturgical observances, the Pope commenced his formal address.

Gaudet Mater Ecclesia – Holy Mother Church rejoices! John XXIII began his Latin address in a firm and clear voice. Unlike most papal speeches and discourses which are written by advisers and specialists, this papal address was written personally by Pope John over the course of many weeks with many revisions. In an image redolent from his peasant background, he described the address as 'flour from my own sack'. Vatican II was 'his' Council and this opening address was going to be foundational in terms of giving the Council inspiration and direction.

The address is best remembered for the way John XXIII hit out at 'the prophets of doom', members of the Roman Curia and others in the Church who on a daily basis carry on as if everything in modern times is heading towards prevarication and ruin. The Pope noted that these people 'are full of zeal but lacking a sense of discretion or measure'. The Pope stated that these times are no worse than previous eras and he reminded his listeners that 'history is the teacher of life'. John XXIII reminded the bishops that Vatican II was to be a fundamentally 'pastoral' Council concerned with bringing the Church up-to-date with the needs of modern times (*aggiornamento*) and seeking the path of Christian unity (ecumenism). Unlike previous Councils, Vatican II was not summoned to argue about 'particular points of theology'. The Pope wanted a new and refreshed presentation of Church teaching to meet the rapidly changing twentieth century. Hence his statement, 'The substance of our central beliefs is one thing and the way in which it is presented is another'.

Members of hierarchy meet. Vatican II 1963, © MDHC Catholic Archdiocese of Melbourne

B. Huebsch, *Vatican II in Plain English: The Council.* Vol 1. Allen, Texas: Thomas More Publishing, 1996, p. 91.

THE FIRST SESSION OF VATICAN II

John XXIII launched the ship. In his opening address he alluded to the fact that there would be debate and disagreement ('everything, even human differences leads to a greater good for the Church') but he made a great act of confidence in the bishops ... 'the Church is now in your hands'. The full implications of this statement were about to be played out in dramatic fashion. Before the Council could get down to business, members needed to be elected for various commissions that would have oversight for the matters to be discussed that at that stage had been prepared in draft form. The Curia had prepared a list of hand-picked candidates that they thought the Council Fathers would simply rubber-stamp. They were seriously wrong. Cardinal Lienart of France followed by Cardinal Frings moved a motion to the effect that the bishops ought to meet in national or regional groups and thus consider the list before voting. Vigourous applause went across St Peter's Basilica and no vote was taken. The bishops streamed out to gather in groups and to seek the opinion of their many theological advisers. Flashpoint number one!

Following this, of all the preparatory schemata or draft documents, the bishops felt that the one on the liturgy was the best prepared and the most suitable for initial discussion. The first issue that came up for discussion was the question of Latin. While Rome had earlier reaffirmed the normative place of Latin in the life of the Church many bishops, especially those in mission countries, felt that the possibility of vernacular languages in the liturgy fulfilled Pope John's charter for the need for adaptation to new circumstances and for a more pastoral approach in debating issues of Church life. As bishops got up to speak, many could not understand each other's Latin! Maximos Saigh, the Melkite Patriarch, stood up and spoke French.

He reminded the assembly that members of the Eastern Churches in communion with Rome are

Council Fathers attending the opening of Vatican II on 11 October 1962, © MDHC Catholic Archdiocese of Melbourne

thoroughly Catholic but do not have Latin as their normative liturgical or theological language. He stated, 'Christ after all spoke the language of his contemporaries ... all languages are liturgical'.

J. O'Malley, *What Happened at Vatican II*. Cambridge, MA: Belknap Press of Harvard University Press, 2008, p. 136.

As the Council got under way and the debates began to focus the international media's attention on the seriousness of some of these debates, a number of bishops and theologians became quite prominent in their comments and advocacy for various Council positions.

- Cardinal Alfredo Ottaviani – secretary of the Holy Office and president of the Preparatory Theological Commission; generally seen as the leading figure of the minority of the Council.
- Cardinal Giuseppe Siri – archbishop of Genoa and member of the Central Preparatory Commission, spokesman for the minority and close adviser to Pope Pius XII. Is alleged to have said that the idea of the Council was John XXIII's 'fifteen minutes of folly'.
- Cardinal Augustin Bea – German Jesuit and brilliant scripture scholar, later to become president of the Secretariat for Christian Unity, a cause very dear to John XXIII's heart. Bea was confessor to Pope Pius XII and helped to shape Catholic openness to critical biblical studies.
- Maximos Saigh – Patriarch of Antioch (Syria) and leader of the Melkite bishops at the Council. Noted for his outspoken comments in terms of reminding Council fathers of the rich, ancient and diverse Eastern and Oriental traditions of the Catholic Church.
- Cardinal Joseph Frings – archbishop of Cologne and leading spokesman for the majority. His young theological adviser at the Council was none other than Joseph Ratzinger (Pope Benedict XVI).
- Cardinal Leon-Joseph Suenens – archbishop of Malines/Brussels, one of the most influential members of the Council and highly influential in the framing of the document *Gaudium et Spes*.
- Cardinal Giovanni Battista Montini – archbishop of Milan, elected as Pope Paul VI in 1963 following the death of John XXIII. Highly gifted thinker who as pope had to hold in tension the many factions of the Council.
- Cardinal Giacomo Lercaro – archbishop of Bologna, leading proponent of liturgical and catechetical renewal after the Council. He was instrumental in co-founding Bologna's Institute of Religious Sciences in the early 1950s in order to promote theological and historical renewal in the Church before Vatican II.
- Archbishop Marcel Lefebvre – French born African missionary, former superior general of the Holy Ghost Fathers and archbishop of Dakak (Senegal). Implacable opponent of many of Vatican II's reforms who was excommunicated in 1988 for illicitly ordaining four bishops without a mandate from the Holy See.
- Edward Schillebeeckz – Belgian Domincan theologian and adviser to Cardinal Alfrink of Utrecht. Leading light in terms of renewing the Church's understanding of the sacraments and Christian anthropology.
- Yves Congar – French Dominican theologian who promoted major ecclesiological renewal for the Church and who was censured by Rome before Vatican II. His ideas gained wide acceptance even in the face of great resistance from the minority.
- Joseph Ratzinger – brilliant young German theologian, professor at Bonn then Munster, theological adviser to Cardinal Frings. Highly influential among the German bishops and generally considered in the vanguard of promoting reform and renewal in theology. As cardinal and head of the Congregation for the Doctrine of the Faith (CDF) in Rome, perceived as putting the 'brakes' on some of Vatican II's reforms.
- Karl Rahner – German Jesuit theologian, under suspicion before the Council but named by John XXIII as consultant to the Preparatory Commission on the Sacraments and personal adviser to Cardinal Koenig of Vienna. A prolific author and highly significant theologian of the twentieth century,
- Marie-Dominique Chenu – French Dominican theologian and historian, founder of 'la nouvelle theologie'– new methods of understanding theology that were highly criticised by Rome before Vatican II.

- Jean Danielou – French Jesuit theologian, early promoter of 'la nouvelle theologie' whose work mainly focused on the Church's relationship to the world. Later appointed a cardinal who was less than positive with some of Vatican II's outcomes.
- Henri De Lubac – French Jesuit theologian and historian, censured before the Council for promoting critical historical studies on the Church, also later made a cardinal.
- John Courtney Murray – American Jesuit theologian, expert on Church/State relations, censured before the Council by Rome but highly influential in the drafting of *Dignitatis Humanae* and expert on issues of religious liberty and conscience.
- Johannes Willebrands – Dutch priest who after Bea was the leading light in the Secretariat for Christian Unity and a giant in the ecumenical world after the Council.
- Jean Guitton – French Catholic layman, philosopher and theologian, close friend and adviser to Paul VI but named one of the first lay auditors by John XXIII. Guitton had met Roncalli during the latter's time as nuncio in Paris.

The first session of the Council met from 11 October until 8 December 1962. There was much discussion over the document on the liturgy as well as the other documents such as divine revelation, social communication and the schema on the Church. After this long eight-week period, no formal votes were taken and all documents remained in draft form subject to further review and input. The first session closed and would reconvene one year later.

DEATH OF THE POPE

In the meantime, prior to the beginning of the second session, Pope John XXIII died on 3 June 1963. There was universal grief and mourning, especially among many non-Catholics and non-Christians, over the death of this much loved pope–genial, warm, humourous and saintly. According to canon law, the Council was technically suspended and the new pope, whoever he may be, was under no obligation to continue what John XXIII had started. On 21 June 1963, Giovanni Battista Montini, the cardinal archbishop of Milan was elected, took the name Paul VI and immediately announced that Vatican II would reconvene.

Vatican City— Pope Paul VI is shown with the late Pope John XXIII during a Vatican audience shortly after he had been designated a Cardinal. At that time he was Archbishop Giovanni Battista Montini of Milan,.
The Advocate, 22 August 1963, © MDHC
Catholic Archdiocese of Melbourne

Further Sessions

It was Paul VI who steered the Council through an increasingly turbulent period of discussion and debate and often had to contend with two opposing forces, commonly known as 'progressives' and 'conservatives', to achieve final agreement on the wording of texts and their implementation in the life of the Church. Sometimes this entailed compromise on a number of theological points. All sixteen final documents of the Council were debated and approved under Paul VI's leadership. Despite the sometimes intense nature of debate, there was a degree of overwhelming acceptance in the final votes.

Pope Paul VI (1963-78)

Did you know?

Despite some intense debate, all the documents of Vatican II received overwhelming support by the bishops. For example:

- Constitution on the Church (*Lumen Gentium*) approved by a vote of 2,151 to 5

- Constitution on the Church in the Modern World (*Gaudium et Spes*) approved by a vote of 2,039 to 75

- Decree on Social Communications (*Inter Mirifica*) approved by a vote of 1,960 to 164

- Decree on the Laity (*Apostolicam Actuositatem*) approved by a vote of 2,305 to 2

- Declaration on Religious Freedom (*Dignitatis Humanae*) approved by a vote of 2,308 to 70.

Vatican II – The Australian Contribution

An ecumenical Council was a totally new experience for the majority of Australian bishops. Bishop James Alipius Goold of Melbourne (1848–86) attended the First Vatican Council in 1869 but by the time of Vatican II, senior bishops such as Archbishop Daniel Mannix (Melbourne) and Archbishop James Duhig (Brisbane) were well into their nineties. This was before the time when bishops submitted their resignation to the Holy See at seventy-five years of age.

Unable to attend in person, Mannix and Duhig sent their respective coadjutor bishops in their place. Cardinal Gilroy of Sydney played an active part as one of the ten Council Presidents. The contribution of the Australian bishops to Pope John XXIII's open invitation for topics to be discussed at Vatican II was a little shallow and uninspiring; however, Archbishop Guilford Young of Hobart had spent many years promoting the idea of participation by lay people in the Mass and the celebration of the liturgy in the vernacular.

The critique (below) by the ninety-five year old Mannix is rather enlightening and somewhat surprising. While there is every chance that a priest or theologian drafted the response, it was despatched with Mannix's signature and with his authority. Mannix's official response was discovered only a few years ago by an Australian researcher in Belgium. Mannix's thoughts are quite prophetic from a number of angles. For example, he highlights the fact that the Church is described too much in institutional and juridical terms and not enough in terms of the Church as a mystery, a sacramental reality that reveals to us God's love and grace throughout salvation history. Mannix emphasises the importance of the word of God in the scriptures, the unique and distinctive place of lay people in the life of the Church and for

Did you know?

At ninety-five years of age, Archbishop Daniel Mannix of Melbourne issued a stern critique of the preparatory document on the Church called De Ecclesia.

The Schema smacks more of a legal document than a spiritual proclamation of religious faith ... for it treats too much of the juridical aspects of the Church, which is almost exclusively represented as a juridical society rather than a participation in the sacrament hidden from the world in God ... The Schema is too preoccupied with the rule and rights of the Church desiring power and authority ... The 'data' of the schema seem to be more recent pontifical sentences rather than the Word of God in Sacred Scripture and the writings of the Fathers ... No other function is seen to be allotted to the laity in the Church than carrying out the commands of the Hierarchy ... It is demanded that the Council affirm more clearly that authority in the Church is humble service and ministry to all ...

J. Murphy, "The Lost (and Last) Animadversions of Daniel Mannix" in *The Australasian Catholic Record*, Vol LXXVI, January (2009), No. 1, p. 70.

all authority in the Church to be seen through the prism of humble service and ministry. Although Mannix died in the middle of the Council and did not participate directly in the debates, these were some of the key issues of Vatican II.

There was a distinctive Australian presence at Vatican II. Fr Michael Costigan was a Melbourne priest and journalist who was present in Rome for each session of the Council. He not only worked with the international media but composed lengthy articles that were published in the Melbourne *Advocate* newspaper, helping priests, religious and lay people 'back home' make sense of some of the complex issues being debated in Rome.

Another distinctive Australian contribution at Vatican II was provided by Rosemary Goldie. Goldie was born in Sydney and had become active in Catholic international lay circles. She was invited to the Council in 1964 as a lay auditor and was the first woman to hold this position. In 1967, Pope Paul VI appointed her as Undersecretary of the newly created Pontifical Council for the Laity; she was the first woman to serve in an executive role in the Roman Curia. Goldie was later also appointed to a professorship at the Lateran University in Rome specialising in pastoral theology. She died in 2010.

Rosemary Goldie, Champion of Catholic Laity, (1916-2010)

Archbishop Simonds Has Audience with Pope

"THE Holy Father spoke affectionately of His Grace Archbishop Mannix, of whom he said he had often heard many and noble things, and sent to him his warm paternal blessing," says His Grace the Most Rev. J. D. Simonds, Coadjutor to Archbishop Mannix, in a letter received from Archbishop Simonds in Rome.

Archbishop Simonds writes:

"On Friday 10 June I had the great privilege of meeting the Holy Father in private audience. I had had the honour of three private audiences with Pope Pius XII, who was very impressive by his dignity and formality, although he was always gracious enough to descend to personal enquiries and kindly individual interest before the interview ended. The experience of meeting Pope John XXIII in his private study is something quite different. He rose to meet me with a most jovial smile and embraced me with a warm expression of welcome. He would not accept the usual ceremonial gestures of homage, but, having

Great Interest in Melbourne Archdiocese

put me sitting beside him in a most brotherly way, he started the interview, which was in the nature of a chat between friends.

"We conversed in French for about twenty minutes, in the course of which chat he laughed heartily at his own jokes. He impresses one as being above all other things a zealous pastor of souls talking with one who is sharing his supreme pastorate in a distant diocese. He took great interest in all I had to say about the progress of the Catholic Faith in the Archdiocese of Melbourne, and was delighted to learn of the generous and militant spirit of the Catholics of our distant Church.

"The Holy Father spoke affectionately of His Grace Archbishop Mannix, of whom he said he had often heard many and noble things, and sent to him his warm paternal blessing.

"After twenty minutes of most enjoyable and warm-hearted chat, the Holy Father said to me: 'Now what can I do to make you more happy as you leave me?' I said that I was always a very happy man, but would be much happier if he gave me his fatherly blessing and sent it also to Archbishop Mannix. He did that with evident pleasure and said that in blessing me he blessed also all the priests, religious and people of our important Archdiocese.

"I then asked his permission to present to him Father Michael Costigan, who acted as my Secretary while I was in Rome, and he graciously consented. The Holy Father himself suggested that a photograph should be taken in his own study and he placed himself between us. We left his genial and fatherly presence carrying with us unforgettable memories of a great Pope and a true Father."

from *The Advocate*, 30 June 1960, © MDHC Catholic Archdiocese of Melbourne

His Grace Archbishop Simonds and Father Michael Costigan, of Melbourne, with Pope John XXIII, after the Archbishop's audience with the Holy Father, *The Advocate* 30 June 1960
© MDHC Catholic Archdiocese of Melbourne

The Second Vatican Council: A Time line

1959

Council events
Jan. 25: Pope John XXIII announces his intention of calling an ecumenical Council.

World events
- Fidel Castro becomes premier of Cuba
- Joan Miró does the murals for the UNESCO Building in Paris
- Formal construction of the Sydney Opera House began
- Donald Bradman retired from cricket.

1960

Council
June 5: Preparatory commissions and secretariats for the Council set up by *motu proprio*, meaning under the Pope's personal authority.

World
- John F Kennedy elected president of the United States
- Three women admitted to the ministry of the Swedish Lutheran church
- Arthur Calwell becomes leader of the Australian Labor Party.

1961

Council
Dec. 25: The Council is formally summoned by the apostolic constitution *Humanae Salutis*.

World
- President John F Kennedy inaugurates the Peace Corps
- U.N. General Assembly condemns apartheid
- Berlin Wall constructed
- Meeting of the World Council of Churches in Delhi
- Yuri Gagarin (U.S.S.R.) orbits the earth.

A Friendly Guide to Vatican II

The Second Vatican Council: A Time line

1962

Council
Sept. 5: Norms and procedures of the Council settled by the apostolic constitution *Appropinquante Concilio*.

Oct. 11-Dec. 8: First session of the Council meets.

World
- Cuban missile crisis
- Australian Army advisers sent to Vietnam to assist in training parts of the South Vietnamese army
- Robert Menzies' *Commonwealth Electoral Act* provided that all Aboriginal Australians should have the right to enrol and vote at federal elections.

Archbishop Mannix with Sir Robert Menzies © MDHC Catholic Archdiocese of Melbourne

1963

Council
June 3: Pope John XXIII dies

June 21: Pope Paul VI elected; announces to continue the Council.

Sept. 29-Dec. 4: Second session of the Council meets.

Issued on Dec. 4: *Sacrosanctum concilium*, "Constitution on the Sacred Liturgy"; *Inter Mirifica*, "Decree On the Means of Social Communication".

World
- Civil rights demonstrations in Birmingham, Ala., culminate in the arrest of Martin Luther King Jr and the calling out of 3,000 troops by President Kennedy
- Nuclear test ban treaty signed by the United States, Soviet Union and Great Britain
- President John F Kennedy assassinated
- Australia signs a trade agreement with Japan
- *Yolngu* people petitioned the Australian House of Representatives with a bark petition after the government sold part of the Arnhem Land reserve on 13 March to a bauxite mining company.
- Daniel Mannix, Archbishop of Melbourne dies.

1964

Council
Jan. 4-6: Pope Paul VI meets Ecumenical Patriarch Athenagoras in the Holy Land.

May 17: Secretariat for Non-Christian Religions established.

Sept. 14-Nov. 21: Third session of the Council meets.

Issued on Nov. 21: *Lumen Gentium*, "Dogmatic Constitution On the Church"; *Orientalium Ecclesiarum*, "Decree On the Catholic Churches of the Eastern Rite"; *Unitatis Redintegratio*, "Decree on Ecumenism".

World
- Martin Luther King Jr wins the Nobel Peace Prize
- Prime Minister Robert Menzies announces the reintroduction of National Service
- The first edition of *The Australian* is published in Canberra.

The Second Vatican Council: A Time line

1965

Council

Sept. 14-Dec. 8: Fourth session of the Council meets.

Sept. 15: Pope Paul VI issues an apostolic constitution, *Apostolica Sollicitudo*, which formulates norms for a new episcopal synod established to assist the Pope in governing the church.

Issued Oct. 28: *Christus Dominus*, "Decree Concerning the Pastoral Office of Bishops in the Church"; *Perfectae Caritatis*, "Decree On Renewal of Religious Life"; *Optatam Totius*, "Decree On Priestly Training"; *Gravissimum Educationis*, "Declaration On Christian Education"; *Nostra Aetate*, "Declaration On the Relation of the Church to Non-Christian Religions".

Issued Nov. 18: *Dei Verbum*, "Dogmatic Constitution On Divine Revelation"; *Apostolicam Actuositatem*, "Decree On the Apostolate of the Laity".

Dec. 4: Prayer Service for Promoting Christian Unity held at St Paul Outside the Walls.

Dec. 7: *Dignitatis Humanae*, "Declaration On Religious Freedom"; *Ad Gentes*, "Decree on the Mission Activity of the Church"; *Presbyterorum Ordinis*, "Decree on the Ministry and Life of Priests"; *Gaudium et Spes*, "Pastoral Constitution on the Church In the Modern World".

Dec. 8: The Second Vatican Council is solemnly ended; extraordinary Jubilee Year proclaimed to familiarise the faithful with the teachings of the Council.

World

■ Pope Paul VI addresses U.N. assembly in New York

■ Prime Minister Menzies commits the first regular military forces to serve in combat in Vietnam

■ Aboriginal Australians gain right to vote in the state of Queensland

■ Charles Perkins leads The Freedom Ride

■ The first drawing of the national service conscription lottery.

Joe McGinness, silent demonstration Adelaide, *The Advocate* 11 May 1967
© MDHC Catholic Archdiocese of Melbourne

Chapter 3:

Implementing Vatican II

The most tangible change that touched the lives of ordinary Catholics as a result of Vatican II was the change in the liturgy. Not only was the liturgy the first document debated by the bishops, it was the one that demonstrated, fairly early, the Church's capacity to change after centuries of apparently no change when liturgical norms and practices seemed timeless and eternal. The first shock for many average Catholics was hearing parts of the Mass spoken in English rather than Latin. Temporary altars were set up closer to the people, the priest faced the congregation rather than having his back to them and the dialogue was now between the priest and the people rather than the priest and the altar boy. Soon churches were redesigned, and altar rails were removed in order to fulfil the principle debated at Vatican II that the liturgy was the action of the people with the priest presiding in the name of Christ. For the first time in centuries, women were allowed to enter the sanctuary area and to proclaim the word of God. Lay people were allowed to assist the priest in the distribution of communion. Communion could now be received under both species. The host could now be received on the hand rather than on the tongue. Many of these practices, although they appeared new and somewhat 'revolutionary', were in fact the recovery of liturgical practices that had been part of the tradition of the Church but long ignored. The Council insisted that the liturgy and the sacraments of the Church are not 'private' functions of the priest where the people sit passively and follow in their missals.

The following quotations from the document on the liturgy (*Sacrosanctum Concilium*) help us to understand the Council's renewed appreciation of the liturgical life of the Church:

The sacred Council has set out to impart an ever-increasing vigour to the Christian lives of the faithful; to adapt more closely to the needs of the age those institutions that are subject to change ... (no.1)

The liturgy is the summit toward which the activity of the church is directed; it is also the source from which all its power flows (no.10).

Pastors of souls must, therefore, realise that, when the liturgy is celebrated, their obligation goes further than simply ensuring that the laws governing valid and lawful celebration are observed. They must also ensure that the faithful take part fully aware of what they are doing, actively engaged in the rite and enriched by it (no.11).

The most obvious changes of the Council related to the liturgy. However, there were significant shifts in other aspects of Catholic life and culture. Vatican II encouraged ecumenical dialogue and discussion. Non-Catholic Christians were no longer called 'heretics' and 'schismatics'. They were called 'separated' brothers and sisters. Gone was the prohibition on Catholics entering non-Catholic churches. Catholics were encouraged to pray with other Christians, discuss disputed points of theology, work together on common social justice projects and move towards dialogue with non-Christian religions. Related to the renewal of the liturgy was the renewed appreciation of the word of God in the life of the Church. Lay people were encouraged to study the scriptures and theology in a critical way. Theological colleges and institutes were no longer places of 'secret men's business'. Lay people, especially lay women and women

> FOR THE FIRST TIME IN CENTURIES, WOMEN WERE ALLOWED TO ENTER THE SANCTUARY AREA AND TO PROCLAIM THE WORD OF GOD. LAY PEOPLE WERE ALLOWED TO ASSIST THE PRIEST IN THE DISTRIBUTION OF COMMUNION. COMMUNION COULD NOW BE RECEIVED UNDER BOTH SPECIES. THE HOST COULD NOW BE RECEIVED ON THE HAND RATHER THAN ON THE TONGUE.

religious went on to gain both undergraduate and postgraduate degrees in theology. The Council deepened within Catholics a concern for social justice and an awareness of some of the tectonic shifts in culture that were occurring throughout the twentieth century which required both some form of dialogue and response from the Church: decolonisation, world poverty, the threat of nuclear war, the changing place of women in society, rapid changes to daily life such as the motor car, the telephone, the television, and the dawning of space exploration. The Council had much to say about these matters. For example:

> In our day, when people are drawing more closely together and the bonds of friendship between different peoples are being strengthened, the church examines more carefully its relations with non-Christian religions ... the Catholic Church rejects nothing of what is true and holy in these religions.
>
> Declaration on the Relation of the Church to non-Christian Religions (*Nostra Aetate*)

> The apostolate of the laity is a sharing in the church's saving mission. Through Baptism and Confirmation, all are appointed to this apostolate. The laity, however, are given this special vocation: to make the church present and fruitful in those places and circumstances where it is only through them that it can become salt of the earth ... evangelization acquires a special character and a particular effectiveness because it is accomplished in the ordinary circumstances of life.
>
> Dogmatic Constitution on the Church (*Lumen Gentium*)

> The church wants the whole world to hear the summons to salvation, so that through hearing it may believe, through belief it may hope, and through hope it may come to love.
>
> Dogmatic Constitution on Divine Revelation (*Dei Verbum*)

> The Vatican Council declares that the human person has a right to religious freedom. Freedom of this kind means that everyone should be immune from coercion by individuals, social groups and every human power ... the Council further declares that the right to religious freedom is based on the very dignity of the human person ...
>
> Declaration on Religious Liberty (*Dignitatis Humanae*)

The thing that is immediately noticeable about the documents is the language used by the Council Fathers. Whereas previous conciliar decrees used harsh and condemnatory language such as '*anathema sit*' (let them be excluded), Vatican II used a form of language that was 'invitational'. The Council documents, while critical of some aspects of modern life, used an altogether different approach in terms of seeking dialogue and mutuality. Professor John O'Malley speaks of the 'rhetoric' of Vatican II, a style of language that held up the Catholic faith for admiration, inspiration and enlightenment. For the first time in the history of the Church, a Council took very serious note of wider contemporary changes to culture and society. The Council began to acknowledge and take notice of the 'global' and therefore changing reality of the Catholic Church. No longer was the Church seen as aloof from history or on some other neat parallel track. The Council helped the church to self-consciously understand that the ancient deposit and patrimony of faith had to, in the words of John XXIII, be expressed in the language and contemporary thought of the day.

Here we get to the nub of some of the difficult issues regarding the implementation and interpretation of Vatican II. The Council resulted in considerable change for the Church especially in the outwards appearance of the Church and the language it spoke. Unlike previous Councils, Vatican II did not fundamentally change or issue any new decrees regarding the central doctrine of the Christian faith. So much of what we call 'change', especially in the area of liturgy, was in fact the retrieval of ancient practices that had fallen into disuse for all sorts of historical reasons. For many centuries, particularly after the Council of Trent, the Catholic Church appeared as a great bastion against societal change, appearing as unchanging, its language and practices timeless and eternal. And yet from the early days of the message of Jesus being preached along the shores of the Sea of Galilee, the Church has constantly changed and adapted itself to new historical circumstances; the eternal message of the Gospel proclaimed afresh and renewed in every historical epoch. This is what John XXIII asked the assembled bishops to be aware of – a new historical epoch or era for the Chu-rch and the world. John XXIII wanted the bishops to 'think big' as opposed to concentrating only on minor administrative matters of church life and governance.

Some major reforms of Vatican II

Changes to the Liturgy

The Mass of the Roman rite, once celebrated only in Latin could now be celebrated also in the vernacular.

Altars were turned around so that priests faced the people.

Sacraments were updated and simplified.

Men and women religious adopted a more modern form of dress.

Bigger role for lay people

Lay people gained a greater role in the celebration of the Mass, including distributing holy communion, which had been strictly the work of priests.

Lay people put their faith into action — to work for peace and unity among ourselves and all Christian churches.

Other religions

Vatican II opened the gates of social activism, freedom of expression and conscience, and a respect for all religions, proclaiming to put an end to centuries-old prejudices and bad blood toward Christian denominations and other religions.

The Scripture

Personal reading and studying of the bible was encouraged.

A greater selection of readings from the Old and New Testaments were chosen for a three-year lectionary cycle.

Documents of Vatican II

In the course of its four year meeting, Vatican II produced sixteen official 'documents' which are the formal legacy of the Council and an insight into the mind of the bishops in terms of addressing specific issues relating to the life of the Church. These had been condensed from the almost seventy preparatory documents or schemata that had been produced in Rome following a worldwide consultation of the bishops. While the final voting patterns demonstrate an overwhelming level of support, the documents were hammered out on the floor of the Council and often reveal intense debates over crucial theological issues that spilled into the public forum. John O'Malley calls Vatican II 'the biggest committee meeting in history' and, as such, the documents reveal many compromises, are sometimes repetitive and vary in quality depending on the level of engagement a particular issue had at the time.

A few important things are to be noted. While Pope John XXIII convoked the Council and witnessed its first session in 1962, none of the sixteen documents were approved during this time even though debate had commenced on the liturgy. All sixteen documents were formally approved and promulgated by Pope John's successor, Paul VI. Like all church documents, there is a certain hierarchy or order of importance regarding the different documents and their level of authority. For example, Vatican II issued four Constitutions, nine Decrees and three Declarations which constitute the corpus of the documents and their specific level of authority. The documents are summarised below in terms of this order, the name of the text in both English and Latin and the date it was approved.

Dogmatic Constitution on the Church
Lumen Gentium
21 November 1964

This document was a significant shift in Catholic ecclesiology. A previous understanding had it that the Church was 'a perfect society' a hermetically sealed reality that was detached from human history and ran in parallel fashion to 'secular' history. *Lumen Gentium* recovered a more sacramental view of the Church describing her as a 'sign and instrument of communion with God and the entire human race'. *Lumen Gentium* describes the Church as the whole People of God, a strong biblical image particularly from the Old Testament, of a chosen and pilgrim people called to witness to the kingdom and to make known God's gift of salvation. It is only after this definition of the People of God that Vatican II elaborates the various indispensable hierarchical offices in the church, ie. pope, bishops, priests, deacons, laity, consecrated religious, etc.

Lumen Gentium

Lumen Gentium highlights the unique and distinctive place of the laity in the Church by virtue of their baptism and that lay people share in the Church's saving mission. (Such sentiments on the importance of lay people are repeated and elaborated further in the specific decree on the Laity). *Lumen Gentium* speaks of the universal call to holiness and the dignity of lay people who share in the universal priesthood of Christ. It is here in *Lumen Gentium* that the word 'evangelization' appears, a word not easily found on the lips of Catholics and often associated with members of Protestant denominations. *Lumen Gentium* holds in high regard members of both non-Catholic denominations and non-Christian religions, stating that the mystery of God's salvific will is not unknown to those who 'seek God with a sincere heart'. This is a major turn-around from previous Catholic attitudes of hostility and use of negative language such as 'schismatics', 'heretics' and 'heathens'. (Vatican II also issued specific documents on ecumenism and non-Christian religions).

Dogmatic Constitution on Divine Revelation
Dei Verbum
18 November 1965

Dei Verbum reminded the Church that 'revelation' was not simply a series of static doctrines and teaching but the revealing of God's salvific will fully in Christ that had been known to the chosen people in the Old Testament. Revelation is about the person of Jesus Christ revealing God's saving love for the world and announcing the presence of the kingdom of God as good news. Jesus Christ is 'both the mediator and the sum total of revelation'.

Dei Verbum paid particular attention to, and elaborated on, the importance of the Word of God in the life of the Church. It recommended that the riches of the scriptures be opened up more widely for the Christian faithful. This was a significant shift for the Catholic Church given that the bible was often the strict domain of the ordained and often associated with Protestant worship. Now Catholics were being encouraged to take up the bible, study the scriptures and use them as a source of prayer. Following the Council, the Church introduced what we now know as the three yearly cycle of lectionary readings to broaden the use of scripture in Catholic worship and sacramental life whereas before Vatican II, the same readings were used every Sunday, year after year. *Dei Verbum* also spoke about the relationship between scripture and tradition, that is the teaching office of the Church, the 'magisterium' is not superior to the Word of God but is rather its servant. While the Church upholds the absolute centrality of the sacraments, especially the Eucharist, the Council called on Catholics to understand that the word of God is also indispensable 'nourishment' for the Christian life.

Dei Verbum also opened up for Catholics a better understanding of the bible in terms of understanding its 'literary forms'. While the Church believes that all the bible is 'the inspired Word of

Dei Verbum

God', not all of the bible can be relied upon for facts and biographical history. Building on decades of scriptural research (mainly by Protestant scholars), the Council affirmed that the truth of faith is often expressed in various types of historical writing, in prophetical and poetical texts and in other forms of literary expression. For example, the four Gospels were written at different times, by different authors, for different audiences each seeking to highlight particular themes of the earthly ministry of Jesus and reflecting different aspects of the life of the early Christian communities following the resurrection.

As is often the case in the Vatican II documents, *Dei Verbum* commences with the Council's express wish that 'it wants the whole world to hear the summons to salvation, so that through hearing it may believe, through belief it may hope, through hope it may come to love'.

Constitution on the Sacred Liturgy
Sacrosanctum Concilium
4 December 1963

This was the first document debated by the Council and the one that had most immediate impact on

Catholics and parish life at the local level. It was the liturgy in particular where Catholics became aware that major changes were occurring at this Council in Rome and things like the liturgy that had remained unchanged for centuries were now going in a very different direction. The change was enormous: from the Latin to the vernacular, from the priest having his back to the people to facing the congregation, the removal of altar rails, the participation of the lay faithful through commentaries and the proclamation of the Word of God, the involvement of women in the liturgy, changes in musical styles and church architecture, lay people actually being allowed up into the sanctuary space once reserved only for the priest and the altar servers, receiving communion under both species and receiving communion from a designated lay person. These changes in such a relatively short period of time appeared as 'revolutionary'. In fact, such practices were not that new or revolutionary but the recovery of ancient practices that over the years had been abandoned due to the increased clericalization of the liturgy. Once again, liturgical scholars had for decades been studying issues of 'participation' in the liturgy, greater 'accessibility' in terms of the vernacular and the idea of 'dialogue' in the liturgy between priest and people and not simply between the priest and altar server.

This was a major shift in Catholic consciousness. For decades, Catholics had been obliged to attend Mass or to 'hear' the Mass with many either saying the Rosary or following the liturgy in their missal. Now the Council was saying that 'the faithful should be led to take that full, conscious and active part in liturgical celebrations which is demanded by the very nature of the liturgy itself'. The Council also insisted on the importance of Christian baptism and a renewed understanding that all sacraments flow from 'the paschal mystery of Christ', that is, his life, death and resurrection.

Pastoral Constitution on the Church in the Modern World
Gaudium et Spes
7 December 1965

This was a truly remarkable and historic document of Vatican II. Unlike all the other documents that had their genesis in some form of preparatory schemata, *Gaudium et Spes* was born on the floor of the Council and was part of the express desire of the bishops to say something about the Church's relationship with the world. Whereas in previous eras, the Church had an often antagonistic attitude to 'the world', at Vatican II the bishops, inspired by Pope John XXIII, wanted to enter into dialogue with the world and the rapid changes of the twentieth century in order to better assist the Church in its mission of salvation.

Gaudium et Spes is remarkable both in its length and breadth. Whereas the other documents of Vatican II speak specifically on religious and ecclesial matters (priesthood, liturgy, divine revelation, religious life, etc), *Gaudium et Spes* covers issues not normally associated with conciliar documents. For example, it deals with the rapid changes in history following the Second World War, urbanization, industrialization, human rights, social justice, world poverty, war and nuclear threat, marriage and the family, conscience, the new cultural conditions of life, the political community, international relations, etc. Never before had a Council of the Church not only addressed so many strictly 'worldly' issues but addressed them in such a positive light. There is no doubt that *Gaudium et Spes* had its genesis in the positive and universal pastoral outlook of Pope John XXIII so beautifully expressed in his opening speech on 11 October 1962. Far from being antagonistic to modern developments, Pope John wanted the Council to learn from the world and engage with the world in order to enhance the Church's proclamation of the Gospel.

Gaudium et Spes is remembered by many people for its prophetic opening statement:

> 'The joys and hopes, the grief and anguish of the people of our time, especially of those who are poor or afflicted, are the joys and hopes, the grief and anguish of the followers of Christ as well'.

However, fifty years after the Council, the Church is called to go deeper into this document in order to truly draw out other riches and insights that perhaps are just as relevant today as they were five decades ago. For example, still in the introductory section we find:

> 'In every age, the church carries the responsibility of reading the signs of the times and of interpreting them in the light of the Gospel, if it is to carry out its task … We must be aware of and understand the aspirations, the yearnings, and often dramatic features of the world in which we live … Ours is a new age of history with profound and rapid changes spreading gradually to all corners of the earth … We are entitled then to speak of a real social and cultural transformation whose repercussions are felt at the religious level also'.

Once again, such sentiments were not entirely new for the Church. In Pope Leo XIII's landmark social encyclical *Rerum Novarum* in 1891, the Church recognised in a subtle way how the changes to the working conditions of life obviously have an effect on social and domestic life as well. Here in *Gaudium et Spes*, the Church acknowledges this more explicitly in terms of wanting to enter into dialogue between faith and modern culture for the mutual benefit of both the Church and the world.

Decree on the Instruments of Social Communication
Inter Mirifica
4 December 1963

This decree on mass media is perhaps the weakest of all the Council's documents. It was written in the context of the wider use and accessibility of modern television technology in the late 1950s and hints at the increasing influence of media in people's lives. On the whole, the Council Fathers endorse this as a sign of progress in modern society and express caution over certain types of media that may prove morally harmful to society, especially the young. The Council encourages priests and lay people to understand the media and to use it effectively in the proclamation of the Gospel and for other forms of pastoral work. The bishops encourage the establishment of national offices to coordinate the work of the Catholic press, cinema, radio and television and for lay people to be suitably qualified to undertake this work.

The Council of course could in no way predict the rapid development of media technology that we have witnessed in recent years and what effect this has on the communication and interpretation of information. The world of instant digital technology and social media has completely transformed the way news and information is both constructed, accessed and disseminated by the general public.

INTER MIRIFICA

Decree on Ecumenism
Unitatis Redintegratio
21 November 1964

The decree on Ecumenism reflects much of the spirit of the Council and John XXIII's specific call to seek the path of Christian unity. For decades, the Catholic Church's limited understanding of ecumenism was for a 'return to Rome', especially from those traditions that had been formed in the wake of the Protestant Reformation. The use of terms such as 'schismatics' and 'dissidents' were not exactly conducive to warm ecumenical dialogue! Now the Council placed ecumenism as a central concern for the Church. Catholics who lived before the Council recall, with some pain, the prohibition of attending baptisms, funerals and weddings of relatives and friends. Catholics marrying non-Catholics could not have the ceremony performed in the church but in the sacristy where the priest would vest before Mass. In the wake of the Council, all this changed.

As a result of the Council, ecumenical dialogue now occurs at the highest international and national levels of the Church involving bishops and theologians reflecting together and discussing many contested points of theology. At the local level Christians now pray together, share Christian worship, study the bible together, participate in ecumenical activities such as social justice projects or the Stations of the Cross on Good Friday. But

Unitatis redintegratio

there are still major stumbling blocks. While many Catholics feel a sense of closeness to Anglicans and the traditions that emerged after the Reformation, there is still less than full agreement on issues regarding the sacraments and the nature of ordained ministry. On the other hand, the Catholic Church while recognizing the validity of the sacraments of the Eastern orthodox tradition, still cannot come to agreement regarding jurisdiction and papal primacy.

While much progress has been made in the field of ecumenical dialogue, some in the Church feel that ecumenism has perhaps lost some momentum since the Council and respectful dialogue reaching a certain point beyond which effective union or reunion is still only a dream.

Decree on the Catholic Eastern Churches
Orientalium Ecclesiarum
21 November 1964

This relatively short decree concerns those distinct eastern Churches that while retaining their own specific liturgical, theological, spiritual and canonical traditions are in fact in full communion with the Holy See. These traditions include Coptics, Chaldeans, Maronite, Melkite and Armenian. While the majority of Catholics around the world belong

Orientalium Ecclesiarum

to the Roman or Latin rite tradition, these other churches of sometimes ancient origin, particularly around the Middle East, have distinctive forms of liturgy, governance and spirituality.

In a country such as Australia, these communities are quite numerous and it is not uncommon for Latin-rite Catholics to attend such churches. However, they often come away with the mistaken notion that they have attended an 'orthodox' ceremony of another denomination without realizing that they have participated in a tradition fully in communion with Rome. These Churches are never to be seen as some form of 'inferior' Catholicism and in fact are to be esteemed as part of a much wider 'catholic' family. The grand entrance procession into St Peter's Basilica at the commencement of Vatican II demonstrated this diversity in terms of some quite distinctive liturgical garments that broke the monotony of the waves of white-mitred Latin-rite bishops!

Decree on the Pastoral Office of Bishops in the Church
Christus Dominus
28 October 1965

It is no accident that the word 'pastoral' is inserted in the title of this document, as indeed it could have been for every document of Vatican II, given Pope John's desire that the Council have an overall pastoral orientation. It was John XXIII's emphasis of his role as pastor and shepherd that underlies *Christus Dominus*. For centuries, popes and bishops often acted like (and looked like) worldly monarchs and feudal lords. John XXIII shifted the emphasis and his style of leadership recovered a servant model, a more biblical emphasis of pope and bishop acting as pastors and shepherds not only of their Catholic flock but also with a pastoral concern for other Christians, those belonging to other religions and those with no discernible faith whatsoever.

Christus Dominus reintroduced the notion of 'collegiality' in the Church. While the Pope is ultimately the head of the Catholic Church and the final source of appeal, all the bishops of the world share with him in the governance of the Church. As a body, the bishops form a college 'with Peter and under Peter' and the Council itself was the concrete embodiment of collegiality at work. An extension of this principle was the formation of the Synod of Bishops, a regular meeting of a representative group of Catholic bishops from around the world with the Pope to consider a particular aspect of Church life. Since Vatican II, such synods have gathered normally every three years to either discuss a particular topic such as the family, religious and laity or to look at the Church in a particular geographical area such as Asia, Africa or the Middle East.

CHRISTUS DOMINUS

Another significant aspect of *Christus Dominus* is the way it positioned the diocesan bishop as the leader of the local church in communion with the Bishop of Rome and not as some form of junior branch manager of a multinational organization. By virtue of their consecration, bishops are successors of the apostles who make present the mystery of Christ's church in a particular geographical area or diocese. They are called to be the leaders, teachers, pastors and point of ecclesial union in that particular diocese.

DECREE ON PRIESTLY FORMATION
Optatum Totius
28 October 1965

This decree contains one of the most repeated phrases of the Second Vatican Council 'adaptation to the new and changing conditions of life'. It is implied in this decree that priestly formation can

OPTATUM TOTIUS

no longer be undertaken in a vacuum or in some form of monastic seclusion from 'the world'. Future priests are to be trained in the various theological disciplines in order to be formed as teachers and shepherds. However, they are also to take account of intellectual and cultural trends in their own particular region of the world so as to better proclaim the Gospel and 'enter into dialogue with the people of their time'. Priests are called to work collaboratively with the lay faithful. This decree is closely related to the following one which treats in a fuller way the ministry and life of priests.

DECREE ON THE MINISTRY AND LIFE OF PRIESTS
Presbyterorum Ordinis
7 December 1965

This decree is much more explicit in terms of helping priests to be aware of the many new challenges that face them in their daily ministry. The Council's reappraisal of the place of the Word of God in the life of the Church demands of priests a better understanding of the scriptures and the changed social/cultural context of their

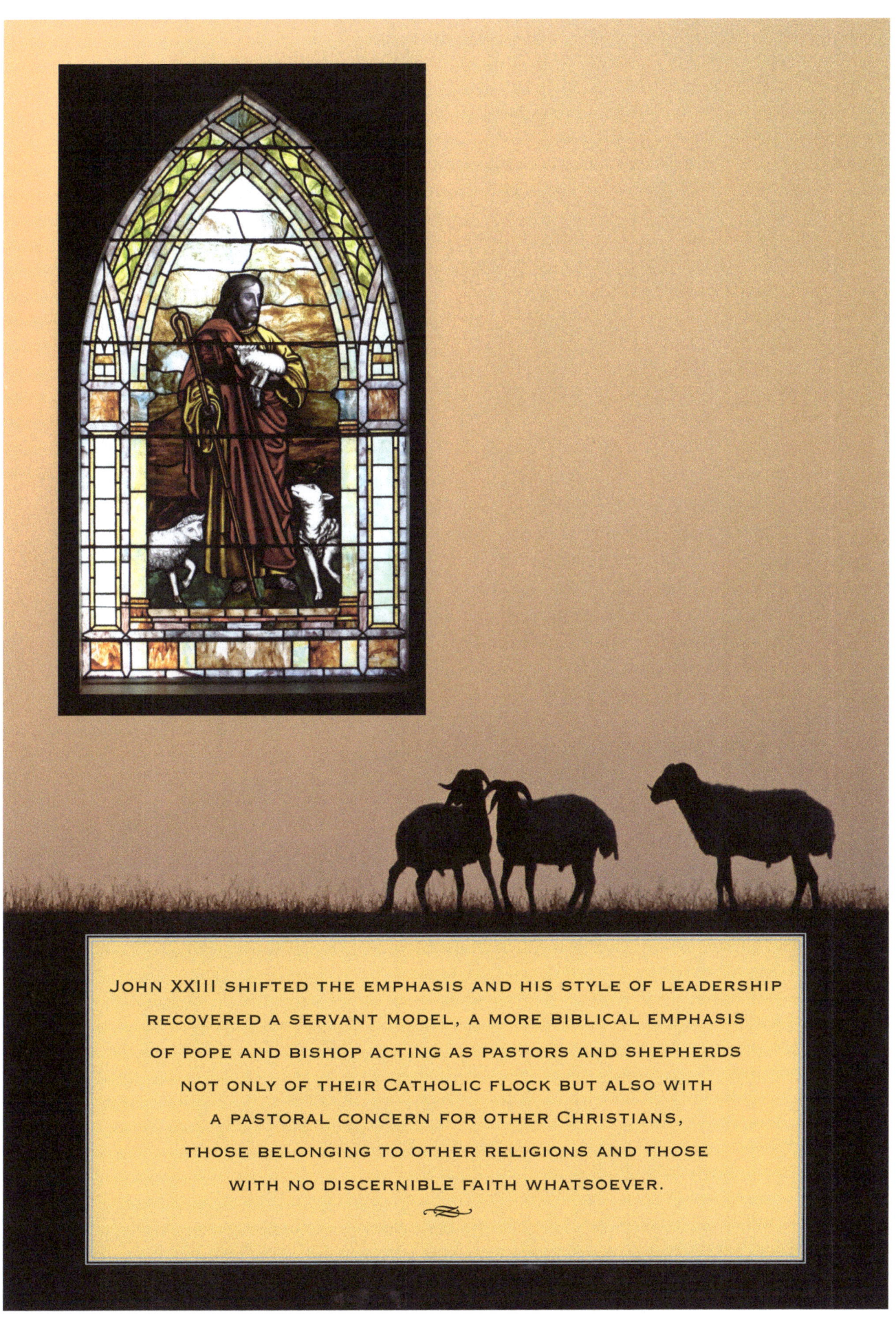

John XXIII shifted the emphasis and his style of leadership recovered a servant model, a more biblical emphasis of pope and bishop acting as pastors and shepherds not only of their Catholic flock but also with a pastoral concern for other Christians, those belonging to other religions and those with no discernible faith whatsoever.

preaching. 'Moreover, the priest's preaching, often very difficult in present-day conditions, if it is to become effective in moving the minds of his hearers, must expound the word of God not merely in a general and abstract way but by the application of the eternal truth of the Gospel to the concrete circumstances of life'.

PRESBYTERORUM ORDINIS

Priests are reminded that they share a sacramental bond with each other and with their bishop, acting as 'co-workers' with the bishop in proclaiming the good news. Hence Vatican II directed that each diocese was to have a senate or Council of priests whom the bishop would consult in assisting his leadership and in planning appropriate pastoral strategies. Priests are called to work collaboratively with lay people 'and to break new ground in pastoral methods under the guidance of the Spirit'.

Decree on the up-to-date Renewal of Religious Life
Perfectae Caritatis
28 October 1965

The most salient feature of this decree is the call for women and men religious to 'go back' to their roots and the original inspiration of their respective founders in order to renew religious life so as to 'adapt to the changed conditions of life and evaluate the contemporary world wisely in the light of faith'. The themes of renewal and adaptation are very strong in this document. Orders, congregations and institutes that were founded centuries ago were being called upon by the Council to renew their customs, traditions and observances in order to adapt to the new demands of their respective ministries and apostolates.

The most radical form of this renewal began with religious dress. Nuns with long flowing habits and almost totally covered faces adopted a more modern form of religious dress. Religious sisters discovered that the original 'charism' of their founder required of them not to be locked behind high convent walls but to minister to the poor and most marginalised of society. Women and men religious, especially those in teaching orders, were given much more freedom to study at secular universities and to branch-out into new ministries beyond Catholic schools, hospitals and orphanages. Interestingly, this decree did not repeat the teaching of the Council of Trent that religious life was a 'superior' state to married life.

Decree on the Apostolate of the Laity
Apostolicam Actuositatem
18 November 1965

This is the document that was perhaps Vatican II's finest hour. Previous Council documents were generally addressed to bishops, priests, religious and

APOSTOLICAM ACTUOSITATEM

PERFECTAE CARITATIS

theologians. Here Vatican II has something specific and powerful to say to the laity of the Church. The laity are recognised for their unique and distinct place in the life of the Church by virtue of their baptism and their universal call to holiness. They share in the universal mission of their Church *in their own right* and not as simple 'helpers' of the clergy. They are called to live their vocation of witness and service 'in the world' and to transform the world by their proclamation of the Gospel. This decree builds on the specific force given to the lay vocation in *Lumen Gentium* and is the result of a specific theology of the laity that had been developed in the Church through movements such as Catholic Action. As a result of the Council, new opportunities began to open up for lay people in terms of studying theology, scripture and liturgy and taking up senior positions of leadership and ministry in the Church.

Decree on the Church's Missionary Activity
Ad Gentes
7 December 1965

This decree expresses a shift in attitude in terms of the Church's missionary activity. Whereas in previous centuries, the Church felt it was evangelizing and bringing western culture to native tribes and pagans, Vatican II affirmed that the proclamation of the Gospel had to be sensitive to local conditions and, more importantly, adapt catechesis so as to be in harmony with the character of local people. Here the Council promotes the idea of dialogue and moves away from forms of European cultural superiority. The richness and beauty of the Gospel is to enter a respectful dialogue with the people and customs of the various parts of the world where the Church's missionary efforts occur.

The decree is a reminder that the Church is essentially missionary by its very nature. The document hints at the fact that many countries at that time were beginning to throw off the yoke of western colonialism and seek their own rightful independence in the international community. This was especially the case in Africa and Asia and the Council encouraged all missionaries to be aware of such circumstances: 'They must approach people with an open mind and heart … and generously accommodate themselves to the different customs and changing circumstances of other peoples'.

Declaration on Christian Education
Gravissimum Educationis
28 October 1965

This is perhaps not the strongest document issued by the Council. Other than reminding parents that they are the first educators of their children, the document does not have a coherent framework other than making general points about Catholic schools and universities. As is often the case, the Council hints at the changing sphere of education in general and how new technology and systems of thought will inevitably change the way people learn and engage with culture.

In many parts of the world, the greatest change in Catholic education occurred as a result of women and men religious not as engaged in Catholic schools as was once the case and the teaching staff in these institutions moving increasingly to qualified lay people. This was certainly the case in Australia and radically changed the make-up of these schools.

Declaration on the Relationship of the Church to Non-Christian Religions
Nostra Aetate
28 October 1965

While this document is in the lowest order of Council authority, it generated much intense debate. It began as a statement of the Church's relationship to Jewish people but was expanded

Nostra Aetate

to include people of various religions around the world. The Council stated that there are elements of 'truth' in these quite diverse religions and that God's love is never denied to those who seek him with a sincere heart. This was a significant shift for the Church that before the Council proudly proclaimed 'no salvation outside the Church' to now saying 'the Catholic Church rejects nothing of what is true and holy in these religions'.

The issue of the Church's relationship to the Jewish people was a 'hot-button' issue at Vatican II, especially after Pope Pius XII's alleged 'silence' in the wake of the Holocaust. The Church rejected any form of discrimination or persecution of the Jewish people which was quite a landmark given that the Church over the years had expressed anti-Semitism in various forms. The Council also rejected the notion of 'deicide', that the Jewish people as a race were responsible for the crucifixion of Jesus.

Declaration on Religious Liberty
Dignitatis Humanae
7 December 1965

Like the previous document, this one on religious freedom likewise caused intense debate on the Council floor because it was turning upside down a previously held attitude of the Church 'that error has no rights'. While claiming the right of religious freedom, the Church affirms that an individual can never be 'compelled' to believe and that, by definition, faith is the human being's free response to God's gift and grace.

Given the acute climate of 'human rights' that was developing at this time, the document states 'People nowadays are becoming increasingly conscious of the dignity of the human person … This Vatican Council pays careful attention to these

Dignitatis Humanae

spiritual aspirations …'. According to the Council Fathers, the right of religious freedom is based on the very dignity of the human person. This was a significant change of attitude for the Church and led some to erroneously believe that the truth of the Gospel was somehow compromised if human beings exercised their freedom to reject it.

Chapter 4:

The Continuing Debates

Understanding the Council that Changed our Lives

It is now fifty years since the commencement of the Second Vatican Council. While the Council was convoked by a pope who was greatly loved and admired and issued documents that used a softer, more pastoral and less harsh form of language, there is no avoiding the reality of conflict and division in the Church since that time and up to the present. While there were major debates on the Council floor, the final documents were approved by an overwhelming majority of bishops. As these documents were released, studied and implemented, there appeared the first signs of tension between the 'letter' of the Council (the documents) and the 'spirit' of the Council, this more pastoral, bridge-building, open-minded attitude that some thought could go beyond the confines of the written word. Pope Paul VI made 'dialogue' the centre-piece of his papacy. But he also used his papal authority to remove some issues from conciliar debate such as priestly celibacy and birth control, and to reserve to himself the implementation of the Synod of Bishops, the consultative body assembled by the Pope every three years to keep alive the spirit of dialogue and discussion evident at the Council. Following the Council, many thought that the Catholic Church might shift on mandatory celibacy. It did not. As the papal commission on birth control continued its discussions throughout the 1960s, expectations were high that the Church might change its position on artificial birth control. It did not. Paul VI in *Humanae Vitae* issued in 1968, reiterated Catholic teaching on this issue. There was immense fallout. Priests and religious resigned en masse from the Church. Many lay people expressed public disagreement. The church was criticised by public figures around the world who were experts in the fields of medicine and international development.

The context of the time was crucial. 1968 was the year of university riots and uprisings around the

> WITHIN THE CHURCH, PAPAL AUTHORITY WAS OFTEN QUESTIONED AND TACKLED.
> AT TIMES, PAUL VI WAS A PONTIFF UNDER SIEGE CAUGHT BETWEEN THE MORE PROGRESSIVE VOICES IN THE CHURCH SOMETIMES CLASHING WITH MORE TRADITIONALIST ATTITUDES.
>
>

world. Young politically enlightened and activist students, attempted to shake off the shackles of authority and seek a more open and democratic forum in public life. A young German professor of theology, Joseph Ratzinger, was greatly shocked at how students took over lecture theatres, occupied senior administration offices and arranged lengthy vigils and sit-ins in defiance of prevailing authority. Such open tensions in society as a result of the sexual revolution, feminism, civil rights and the development of a vocal and politically aware youth culture came to also afflict the Church. Dialogue, friendship and the pastoral openness of Vatican II collided with the social, cultural and political upheavals of the 1960s.

Within the Church, papal authority was often questioned and tackled. At times, Paul VI was a pontiff under siege caught between the more progressive voices in the church sometimes clashing with more traditionalist attitudes. At the Council, this tension achieved a degree of respectability. By the 1960s and 70s, there was open defiance. As young priests and religious entered more into dialogue with their changing culture, obedience to the wishes of religious superiors appeared to become a commodity. Some felt that the Council had not gone 'far enough' to embrace the modern world; others felt that too much 'embracing' was the cause of the upheavals of the 1960s. As electric guitars and rock bands made their way into the Catholic liturgy, many longed for the days of Latin Masses and solemn exposition. Both the church and the world were caught in a period of turmoil and cultural flux, both entering challenging and uncharted waters.

Individuals such as Joseph Ratzinger, now Pope Benedict XVI, are some of the few surviving participants of the Council. (Ratzinger was a theological adviser to Cardinal Frings and not a Council Father as such. The late Pope John Paul II was a young bishop at the time of Vatican II). Following Ratzinger's rise to head the Congregation for the Doctrine of the Faith in Rome, he was often seen as one who put the 'brakes' on much of the openness of Vatican II. He has often stated that ground-breaking documents such as *Gaudium et Spes* were a little too optimistic about the human condition, human nature and the idea of ongoing progress and development in world affairs. His election to the papacy in 2005 was watched carefully by many people, especially with regard to what he would say about Vatican II and its interpretation, a Council that he contributed to in no small way.

Ratzinger's election in 2005 coincided with the fortieth anniversary of Vatican II's conclusion (1965). In his end-of-year address to the Roman Curia, the Pope noted this historic coincidence and went on to say:

> ... it all depends on the correct interpretation of the Council or – as we would say today – on its proper hermeneutics, the correct key to its interpretation and application. The problems in its implementation arose from the fact that two contrary hermeneutics came face-to-face and quarrelled with each other. One caused confusion, the other, silently but more and more visibly, bore and is bearing fruit.
>
> One the one hand, there is an interpretation that I would call 'a hermeneutic of discontinuity and rupture'; it has frequently availed itself of the sympathies of the mass media, and also one trend of modern theology. On the other hand, there is the 'hermeneutic of reform,' of renewal in the continuity of the one subject-Church that the Lord has given us. She is a subject that increases in time and develops; yet always remaining the same, the one subject of the journeying People of God.
>
> The hermeneutic of discontinuity risks ending in split between the pre-conciliar Church and the post-conciliar Church.

M. Lamb & M. Levering, (eds.),
Vatican II: Renewal within Tradition.
New York: Oxford Univeristy Press, 2008, ix-xv.

While the decisions made in Rome during the course of Vatican II achieved overwhelming support by the bishops of the time, the implementation of those decisions over the last five decades have been a cause of major debate and division in the Church. This is more than just a demarcation dispute between 'progressives' and 'conservatives' — the former embracing more of the 'spirit' of the Council with the latter concentrating on the written 'law' of Vatican II. Pope Benedict was addressing his words to a fundamental issue regarding the Church's very essence and identity. Was there some form of change at Vatican II? By all accounts, both sides of the debate would answer with a resounding 'Yes!' The question is whether this change amounted to some form of 'rupture' or 'discontinuity' to the extent that the Church *after* the Council looked, sounded and spoke quite differently to the Church *before* the Council. As a theologian, Pope Benedict holds the need for change in tension with the belief that the one mystery of the Church continues to develop as opposed to this sense that at the Council one historical reality (the Church) was demolished and another reconstructed in its wake.

Pope Benedict's address in 2005 was felt by many to be a direct rebuttal to a particular form of historical interpretation and scholarship on Vatican II that had emanated from the 'Bologna school', a largely lay-run group of international scholars that form part of the Institute of Religious Sciences – John XXIII Foundation (*Istituto per le Scienze Religiose – Fondazione Giovanni XXIII*). The Institute was co-founded in the 1950s by the Italian historian, the late Professor Giuseppe Alberigo. He and his fellow researchers have promoted an interpretation of Vatican II that highlights the Council as an epochal event or shift for the Catholic Church. The Council was so significant that while the Church remained faithful to its ancient patrimony of faith (as emphasised by Ratzinger), the nature of change was so significant that as a result of the Council, it was no longer 'business as usual' for the Catholic Church. There was a considerable shift in language, customs and practices. Was this change so great that one can now speak of 'rupture' or 'discontinuity' between the pre and post Vatican II Church? This remains at the heart of the many debates in recent decades.

The Nature of the Change

As mentioned earlier, the first document debated by the bishops and the first area of major change for the Church was the liturgy. The Latin liturgy that a previous generation had grown up with had remained largely unchanged for almost 400 years since the Council of Trent. The changes introduced at Vatican II were revolutionary in the eyes of many and appeared to up-end centuries of established Catholic practices and customs. But a deep and penetrating reading of history demonstrates that many liturgical norms introduced at Vatican II were not new, novel or revolutionary but in fact the retrieval – the going back into history, deep into the Catholic tradition – of past practices that had fallen into disuse. Speaking in the vernacular (not Latin), communion on the hand, communion from the cup, having the priest face the people, removal of the altar rails to enable all lay people to enter the sanctuary area – these are all practices that were 're-introduced' by Vatican II. While on the surface they may appear as novel, a form of rupture or evidence of discontinuity, these elements are evidence of decades of liturgical scholarship and research that were occurring long before Vatican II. In fact, what is known as the 'liturgical movement' of the late nineteenth century was actually given some impetus by Pope St Pius X (1903–14) who lowered the age for the

> Pope John stated he wanted to change, not so much the ancient deposit, but the way the Church went about proclaiming its message by adapting itself to the new historical circumstances that were emerging in the twentieth century.
>
>

reception of First Communion and encouraged frequent, even daily, reception of the Eucharist by the faithful. Even in the reform of Church music, Pius X encouraged liturgical participation and accessability to the sacraments by the faithful.

As John O'Malley points out, one of the difficulties of reading the Vatican II documents is that the Council, by its very nature, was to be the guardian and protector of the Church's ancient deposit of faith. Unlike previous Councils, Vatican II defined no new church dogma or teaching such as the nature of Christ's humanity and divinity or any other of those central tenets of faith defined in the Creed. But by using a new form of language or 'rhetoric', the Council *did* make some major changes to the life of the Church. The Council documents did not 'change' the Church as such, but did set the Church in a new direction. But nowhere in the documents is this stated explicitly. For example, you arrive at the train station on a particular platform expecting to go to X. Suddenly an announcement is made: 'Passengers please note. The train on platform 1 is not going to X but to Y.' You now know that the train is going in another direction. It has been *explicitly* stated. But this was not the case at Vatican II. Changes were made without explicit acknowledgement. In fact, ambiguities emerged in areas such as the liturgy. For example, *Sacrosanctum Concilium* states 'The use of the Latin language ... is to be preserved in the Latin rites'(no.36.1). 'But since the use of the vernacular ... may frequently be of great advantage to the people, a wider use may be made of it ...'(36.2). And further along the document states, 'Even in the liturgy the church does not wish to impose a rigid uniformity in matters which do not affect the faith or well-being of the entire community. Rather does it cultivate and foster the qualities and talents of the various races and nations'(37). So, there will be Latin and, on the other hand, there won't be Latin! A perfect scenario to argue the case either way and a perfect storm for clashing interpretations of the Council.

Another example was the Council's positive attitude to 'the world' in documents such as *Gaudium et Spes*, especially to the secular, non-Catholic and non-Christian reality of human history. For centuries, popes had denounced freedom of conscience, freedom of religion, freedom of the press, the separation of Church and state. Vatican II adopted the language of mutuality, dialogue, brotherhood, and non-Catholics were no longer castigated for being 'heretics' and 'schismatics'. A change in attitude, language and direction was evident but none of the documents announce, like the train station analogy, 'Attention passengers, this train is now departing in another direction'. The Council, in an authoritative way, reinterpreted centuries of antagonistic church teaching against 'the world' without explicitly saying as much.

The documents of Vatican II need to be held in tension and interpreted in context. The best context (historically) is to return to Pope John's opening speech on 11 October 1962. At no stage in that opening speech did John XXIII state what Pope Benedict fears the most – the demolition of one ancient ecclesial mystery and reality and the construction of a new type of 'church' more in conformity with the modern world. Pope John stated he wanted to change, not so much the ancient deposit, but the way the Church went about proclaiming its message by adapting itself to the new historical circumstances that were emerging in the twentieth century:

> Ecumenical Councils like this, whenever they gather, are an occasion for the celebration once again of the unity between Christ and the Church. They lead to a more clear announcement of the truth, to guidance for people in everyday life, and to the strengthening of spiritual energy for the sake of goodness ...
>
> I confidently trust that under the light of this Council the Church will become richer in spiritual matters and, with this new energy, will look to the future without fear. In fact, by bringing itself up-to-date where needed, the Church will make people, families and whole nations really turn their minds toward divine things ...
>
> In fact, at the present time, Divine Providence is leading us to a new order of human relations which, by the very effort of the people of this time, is directed toward the fulfilment of God's great plans for us. Everything, even human differences, leads to greater good for the Church ... The greatest concern of this Council is this: that the sacred and central truths of our Christian

faith should be guarded and taught more effectively ... but we will be attentive to these times, to the new conditions and new forms of life present in the modern world which have opened new arenas of work for Catholics. So while the Church is mindful of marvellous human progress, it is also eager to remind people that God is the true source of wisdom and beauty.

Having said this, it is clear that much is expected of us here regarding the passing on of the doctrines of the Church, as we have done without fail for twenty centuries, despite occasional difficulties in this regard. The important point of this Council is not, therefore, a discussion of one article or another of the fundamental teachings of the Church; a Council would not be needed for such work. Instead, the work of this Council is to better articulate the doctrine of the Church for this age. This doctrine should be studied and expounded through the methods of research and literary forms of modern life.

Here is a key distinction on which our work is based: The substance of our central beliefs is one thing, and the way it is presented is another. It is this latter presentation of the faith with which we are concerned here, and our approach to this will be a thoroughly pastoral one.

But today we prefer to make use of the medicine of mercy rather than that of severity. We meet the needs of the present day by demonstrating the validity of our teachings rather than condemning others ... That being so, the Catholic Church in this Council desires to show herself as the loving mother of all: benign, patient, full of mercy and goodness toward all who are separated from her.

We open here the fountain of our life-giving doctrines which allow all people to understand their real dignity and purpose. Finally through our members, we spread Christian charity, the most powerful tool in eliminating the seeds of discord and in establishing harmony, peace and unity.

B. Huebsch, *Vatican II in Plain English: The Council.* Vol. I, Allen, Texas: Thomas More Publishing, 1996, pp. 85-95.

At no stage in this address did Pope John hint that the purpose of the Council was to demolish some old ecclesial bastion and raise up a totally new and modern church entity. His sense of history and respect for history was too rich and profound. However, he was absolutely clear that a particular 'style' of Catholicism which had been in operation since the Reformation, the Enlightenment, the French Revolution and the fall of the Papal States was perhaps not the most effective way of preaching and living the Gospel in the twentieth century. Pope John's address was an historical shake-up addressed to the bishops and the whole Catholic world. It was no longer 'business as usual'.

www.ingramcontent.com/pod-product-compliance
Lightning Source LLC
Chambersburg PA
CBHW061059170426
43199CB00025B/2944